MOONBEAM

A BOOK OF MEDITATIONS FOR CHILDREN

For Eleanor, who is my light

MOONBEAM

A BOOK OF MEDITATIONS FOR CHILDREN

Maureen Garth

HarperCollins*Publishers*

HarperCollins*Publishers*

First published in Australia in 1992
by HarperCollins*Publishers* Pty Limited
ABN 36 009 913 517
A member of the HarperCollins*Publishers* (Australia) Pty Limited Group
www.harpercollins.com.au

HarperCollins*Publishers*
25 Ryde Road, Pymble, Sydney, NSW 2073, Australia
31 View Road, Glenfield, Auckland 10, New Zealand
77-85 Fulham Palace Road, London W6 8JB, United Kingdom
2 Bloor Street East, 20th floor, Toronto, Ontario M4W 1A8, Canada
10 East 53rd Street, New York NY 10022, USA

National Library of Australia Cataloguing-in-Publication data:

Garth, Maureen.
Moonbeam: a book of meditations for children.
ISBN 1 86371 142 2.
1. Meditation. 2. Meditations. I. Title.

Design by William Hung
Cover design by John Canty
Cover illustration by John Canty
Typeset in Galliard by EMS Typesetting
Printed in China by Everbest Printing on 90gsm Woodfree

20 19   07 08

Contents

Introduction

Why Children Should Meditate

Children are our lifeblood, the essence of our future. What we put forth to a child, be it positive or negative, will be incorporated into that child's persona. Therefore, it is essential that we place high importance on the positive aspects of life and personality, rather than the negative. Meditation is one way of doing this.

Children would benefit greatly from learning the art of meditation. It is not only helpful as an aid for creative visualization but promotes tranquility. It is a marvellous tool to pacify and deal with emotions which children do not understand.

All of us need to have time to ourselves, time to go within, to feel our essence. Training our children to do this in the early stages of their life could help them, not only throughout their childhood and maturing years, but also during their adult life.

Meditation has been an important part of my life for many years. The gentle art of going within for the answers to problems has helped me through difficult phases. It not only helped me in problem-solving, but I found I became calmer, more peaceful and able to cope.

If we can teach our children how to meditate so that it becomes a natural part of their lives, we will be looking at future adults more centred and more aware. They will be able to draw from their innermost being the necessary resources to carry them through the difficulties life can present.

Children respond to meditation in a natural way. Their minds are very flexible, absorbing and dealing with everything around them. The first five years of life are full of concentrated learning. Children learn to sit, to crawl, to walk, to speak, to co-ordinate, to read, to dance, to play, to interact, to write. All these skills, which will carry them forward, are learned during this short period of time.

If meditation were included in this vital early stage, it would become a skill that could help children throughout their lives. They would use meditation as they use their speech, their communication skills. It would be an integral part of their being and as natural as breathing.

Why I Started Meditation With My Daughter

In my first book, *Starbright - Meditations for Children*, I placed a lot of importance on the necessity for starting the meditations as early as possible. I started with my daughter, Eleanor, when she was three years of age by doing simple visual exercises to quieten her at night. Although she slept well, she had an occasional nightmare. A nightmare is a terrible experience, both for the child and the parent. The child shakes and trembles while the parent wonders what has caused the distress. Is it something he or she has done? What is the child seeing in the waking hours to cause such troubled nights?

Because of my concern, I gave Eleanor a Guardian Angel to make her feel safe. I explained how the wings of the angel would go around her so she would feel protected and secure. I then placed Eleanor in a garden and drew a mental picture for her of what could be in her garden: perhaps lots of animals, perhaps a boat she could climb into, or a cloud to float on.

These exercises grew and grew as time progressed until a theme emerged which I call the Star Prelude. I gave Eleanor a Star and I brought its light down throughout her body; her Guardian Angel was there; I filled her heart with love; I gave her a Worry Tree where she could place anything of concern. Then I would take her into her garden.

Eleanor loved these times so much she wouldn't sleep until I had told her the meditation for the night. It became more than just telling her a story or meditation. We achieved a more complete way of bonding than I had experienced before, and a very beautiful one.

The meditations also tested my skills as a story-teller. I had never considered myself to be imaginative and never as a teller of tales, yet, when I sat on the edge of Eleanor's bed, the images flowed. I always started with the Star, the Angel, the Heart, the Worry Tree, the entrance to the garden. I would not have any idea what would follow nor what I would say. But when I opened the gate for Eleanor, I always saw something which would give me the story for the night. Sometimes it would be just one thing, say a cloud drifting by. Once I mentioned the cloud, other images would unfold, such as the cloud having reins and coming down to pick her up and take her off into the heavens. I was going into a state of meditation, too, so that the images I saw came from my subconscious.

In *Starbright* I included a number of meditations I had used with Eleanor and also with many children who had stayed overnight. These children still ask me to do a meditation for them when they stay, even if they have not been with us for some time. And they remember the theme I used before. I find it interesting that, in today's hustle and bustle, the children remember the quiet time they experienced during the meditation and wish to enjoy it once more.

The meditations in this book are, as in *Starbright*, only an indication of what you can do. There is no set format. You must feel comfortable with what you are doing and put the meditations into your own words, not mine. The ideas in the meditations might spark off scenes that you might want to explore with your child or children.

Whatever I write is for guidance only and to suggest to your subconscious what you could say, not what you should say.

How To Begin

Each meditation starts with the Star (see page 19), the focal point for setting up the conditions for the meditation. Indeed, the Star is an integral part, the point where the relaxation and visualization starts. The Star is followed by the Angel—or you might prefer to say a wise person—which in turn can be followed by the Worry Tree (if you feel it is necessary). You then do the Meditation you have selected—perhaps The Snow Flakes or The Elphinites. Do whatever you feel is appropriate to the mood of the child or children, or even to yourself.

Although I use a Star as the focal point, you might prefer to use the Moon or perhaps the Sun. It does not matter which; the important thing is to give your child something to focus on. For relaxation and visualization, it is as easy to bring the light down from the Sun or Moon as a Star.

If you use the Moon, for instance, you could say that the Moon's fingers are spreading out over the world so that everyone can see in the night, but there is one special Moonbeam that is coming down just for your child. That Moonbeam is filled with glitter, little sprinkles of which are touching all parts of the body, making it glow in the night.

And if it is the Sun you have selected, you could speak about how the Sun is a golden ball in the sky, filled with warmth and light. A large shaft of sunshine is dancing down to the child's bed where it is caressing and embracing her or him, filling every part of the body with the Sun's rays. *You* must choose the vehicle with which you feel the most at ease, be it the Sun, Moon, or the Star.

For Teachers

I taught meditation at Eleanor's Infant School, which proved to be an interesting experience for several reasons. Very few schools, to my knowledge, encourage meditation. Eleanor's teacher, Helen, who was also the Head Mistress, said she would like me to introduce meditation as a trial. So, it was a first for me, a first for the children, and a first for the school.

The children were excited when they were asked to sit in a circle in order to meditate. I explained that we were trying something new with them and that meditation was like story-telling, only they would have their eyes closed while I drew a story in their minds.

I did the Star Prelude—the light from the Star, the opening of the heart, the Guardian Angel, the Worry Tree, the Garden, and then one of my stories. From the time I started, we noticed that some children immediately went into a relaxed state and stayed motionless for the duration of the meditation. Others fidgeted. They could not sit still and had trouble keeping their eyes closed.

The children who went deeply into meditation, and stayed, happened to be the better students. The ones who fidgeted were children whose attention span was limited and who had difficulty concentrating in the normal course of learning.

Over the next few weeks, I spent time talking with the ones who could not settle. They were not sure what they were supposed to see nor what was expected of them. I explained that they might be able to see, in their imagination, what I was talking about and, if they could not, they might see something else they might want to tell me about.

What surprised both Helen and me was that the children who were having the most difficulty with their studies were improving. They were able to think processes through, which was not possible before. The quality of their stories improved and showed a far better use of imagination.

At that time, I also helped the children "publish" their stories.

They dictated them from their handwritten books and I typed them. Prior to learning meditation, their stories had been about their families, picnics, bikes, etc., with little exercise in imagination, except for the few who naturally visualized well. Again Helen and I were surprised to find that the content of their stories changed and became more colorful, more imaginative, and more creative.

Anything that can free a child's mind should be used. We end up being bound by restrictions, which we must accept to get through life, but our minds should be free and active. Problem-solving becomes easier if the mind can see around corners instead of existing in the limited space to which we sometimes condemn it.

When I do meditations at night, I leave Eleanor at a place in the garden where I feel she will drift into sleep.

In the classroom, you would take the children to a place in the meditation that you feel is right, saying, "I am going to be quiet now and leave you for a while. Let your mind be free. You are very safe and I will bring you back shortly." Leave them in their meditation for approximately five or ten minutes, according to their attention span, then bring them back out of the garden, gently closing the gate behind them. Take them past the Worry Tree, wrap them up in a golden cloak, and tell them to open their eyes when they are ready.

After the meditation, ask each child what they saw or did. You will be surprised at what they come out with. Some see other worlds, some play with animals, some look for the pot of gold at the end of the Rainbow meditation (which is in *Starbright*). One girl said she saw "space" and described it beautifully. Her classmate, who was very much into intergalactic travel, snorted and said, "Don't be silly, you can't go into space without your space suit and helmet."

Some children have a lot to relate; others are a bit shy of saying anything. If they were meditating for a short time at the start of each day rather than once a week, it would free them up immensely. I understand that if meditation is used prior to study, the study process is easier to assimilate.

The Worry Tree is important (see page 22). Children have many concerns we are not aware of. There could be sibling rivalry, dissension in the home, problems with school-friends. How often have we heard that phrase, "I'm not going to be your friend any more", and how often have we had to dry the resultant tears.

The Tone Of Voice

You might think when you read the meditations, that they are not very long. Please remember that when you are speaking, you will do so in a very slow, relaxed voice, pausing to let the scene sink in, so that the child, whose eyes are closed and who is focusing inward, can easily visualize and feel the scene. The way you use your voice is very important. You will find it best to drop your voice by a few tones, speaking more and more slowly, with a soothing quality. There is something hypnotic about a voice which is low and relaxed.

Some of the meditations are longer than others. If you are tired, select a short one. I have found that the children are not concerned with the length, only with the fact that *you* are doing it for *them*.

Although I call them meditations, you might prefer to call them stories. This really is not important, it is only a name. The main thing is that you will be sharing a unique experience with your very special child.

Comments From Children

I am including some comments I received about my first collection of meditations, *Starbright*, which are of interest:

Emma, 6 years old—the following morning she related to

her mother what happened in her garden and then stated, with small hand on hip, "...but Mummy, my Guardian Angel does not like me." "Why not?", asked Mother. "Well, I asked him to turn off my bedroom light and he wouldn't," she said quite indignantly. Mother gently explained that Guardian Angels do not do the physical things that we can do for ourselves. Emma now has a Boy and Girl Angel.

David, 5 years old—the angel is a Guardian Angel because he looks after the garden (he thinks it is a Gardening Angel).

Another of David's comments amazed his Mother. He became quite distressed about the Worry Tree and worried what would happen to the tree, and asked, "How can the Worry Tree put up with all my worries?" This shows that we really do not know what worries go on in small heads. His Mother wrote, "...*Starbright* has made a huge difference with David. He now sleeps through the night..."

Paul, 7 years old—at such an early age, Paul was worrying about whether he would have a job at 20, whether he would be married at 20, and whether he would own his own home at 20. Within a week of using *Starbright*, his mother noticed a profound difference. He felt more secure and less concerned. This would have worked on several levels: the Guardian Angel making him feel protected, the Worry Tree, and the security of the garden, plus the continued personal contact of the parent taking him through his meditation. Paul also worried about what people thought of him and would not play sport. He is now feeling more secure within himself and is now involved in several sports, including soccer.

Joshua, 5 years old—told his grandfather that *Starbright* is the "book of imaginings".

Christopher, 7 years old—told his mother he wanted his own book. He did not want to share the one she was reading from!

Samantha, 4 years old—her mother borrowed the book from a friend for one night. Mother was sent off in the morning with strict instructions to return with their own copy as she wanted the "Animals" to be told to her that night.

I have also heard of children who know the meditations backwards, and you do not dare miss out on a word! Or they will tell you.

Comments From Adults

I have had some interesting responses from parents or grandparents who have used *Starbright*. They say they too have received many benefits from the meditations or stories.

Flora, 62 years old—a grandmother who says the meditations transport her back in time. She finds peace, tranquility and a sense of spirituality from these meditations.

Eve, 82 years old—Eve lives in England and is also a grandmother. She finds that if she cannot sleep, she brings the light from the Star down and either reads one of the meditations or recalls one to mind and drifts off peacefully.

Robert, late twenties—a young parent, has found that he receives as much from what he reads as his children do.

Rhonda, early thirties—she likes to meditate but has found that the light from the Star increases the intensity of her meditations.

Elias, mid thirties—bought *Starbright* for himself as he loves visual guided meditation. He caught the ferry home, ran into a friend who invited him to dinner, and was then asked to read to the children. Elias read from *Starbright* and was not allowed to take the book out of the house. Elias has since bought his own autographed copy.

Many parents have told me that they also drift into the meditative state with their children. This brings to parents the added bonus of feeling more peaceful and tranquil than before they started.

Using The Mind

Using these meditations with children is not the same as reading stories to them. Reading is passive. Children do understand and become involved in what you are reading, but, in a guided meditation, they become actively involved. Reading a story and reading a meditation are different functions. Reading stories to children is a must because it helps the child to learn to read and spell, but meditation enables the mind to become free, to explore.

Each meditation has its own distinctive theme and gives children the opportunity to experience it. They climb mountains; they become a snow-man; they feel the warmth of fur against their skin; they fly without the benefit of a plane; they visit the Queen; they visit Disneyland; they go to the moon. There are so many things they can do, and all these things must bring their imagination to the fore. They can create these scenes in their minds and feel the sensations they bring. In other words, they participate in the meditation.

Do Children Grow out of These Meditations?

Eleanor still loves all the ones that are included in *Starbright*. I started formulating those meditations when she was three and have kept using them, plus the ones in this book, ever since.

I still remember the first time I did the Panda Bear meditation and the look of sheer joy on her face when I described the texture of the fur and how the Panda Bear would give her a big, big cuddle. I did this meditation again a few weeks ago, and there was the same reaction—joy and pleasure. She loves being a fairy—she loves to fly—she loves to be with people—she loves her special garden.

Eleanor was born in July 1981 and I think these meditations will stay with her for years to come. Mind you, I shall certainly be thinking up some new ones for her, but the old ones become like evergreens—always wanted and loved.

How to Meditate

Meditation is a time for reflection and contemplation, a time to go within. It is not beyond the reach of anyone, provided they take the time and create the opportunity.

Meditation is very simple: you need to sit quietly either on your own or with a group of people (it is best to sit in an upright chair—if you make the chair too comfortable, you may fall asleep). Wear loose clothing for comfort but if that is not possible, loosen anything which is tight around the waist or neck so that you do not feel these restrictions. Try not to cross your arms and legs as this can lead to discomfort.

You might like to have soothing music in the background or you might prefer silence. Sometimes I like to fix a scene in my head, such as the garden in which I place the children. Other times my mind is like a blank screen ready to receive whatever images happen to cross it.

Beta is our normal conscious level, the level at which we work in our daily lives. When we go into a meditative state we are going into Alpha, which enables us to create scenes and images on the screen of our mind. There are also the levels, Theta and Delta, which we can attain as we go more deeply into the meditative state. Most of us work very well within Alpha, and come back feeling refreshed and renewed.

It is up to the individual to decide how long to spend in meditation. If you can only spare five or ten minutes that can be ample. To feel the full benefit, however, twenty minutes is better because meditation can promote calmness, relax tension, and give relief from anxiety as you become detached from your problems. Your problems will not necessarily go away, but meditation can be beneficial to the way you handle those problems. Sometimes the solution comes when we take the time to sit quietly.

Meditation is a very soothing, relaxing way of coping with the stress and anxiety of daily life. Many doctors recommend meditation as a wise and good practice for their patients. It is a relaxing and pleasant way to spend such a short period of time, and one that has many benefits.

The Star Prelude

I WANT you to see above your head a beautiful, beautiful Star. This Star is very special to you as it is your very own Star. It can be any color you like— you might see it as being a purple star, or perhaps a pink one—or blue—or yellow—or is it a speckled star? Or a silver one? Because it is your very own Star, it can be any color or colors you choose.

This special Star is filled with white light, lovely white light that shimmers and glows. I want you to see this light streaming down towards you until it reaches the very top of your head. And now I want you to bring this pure light down through your head and take it right down your body until your whole body is filled with this glorious white light.

I want you to feel the light going down your arms, right down, until you feel it reaching your hands and going into each and every finger.

Feel that light going down the trunk of your body, down until it reaches your legs, and when you feel it there, take it right down until it comes to your feet. Then feel the light going through each toe.

I now want you to look into your heart and to fill your heart with love for all the people and animals in the world. They are your friends, be they large or small. Can you see your heart getting bigger and bigger? It's expanding because you have so much love in your heart for all these people and the animals, and of course for yourself.

Now your Guardian Angel is waiting to wrap golden wings of protection around you before taking you into your garden. The Angel's wings are very large and very soft, just like down. Everyone has their own Guardian Angel and that Guardian Angel takes care of you and protects you always, so you are never alone. It's important to remember this and to know that you have someone who looks after you with love and care.

Your Guardian Angel is now going to take you to a garden that is your own special place, but before you enter I want you to look at the large tree that is outside. This tree is called the Worry Tree. I want you to pin on this tree anything that might worry you—perhaps you have had some arguments at school, or maybe you are having difficulty with your school work. This tree will take any worries at all, be it with your friends or your family. This tree accepts anything that you would care to pin there.

Your Guardian Angel is now opening the gate for you to enter, and as you go in you find the colors are like nothing you have seen before. The beauty of the flowers, the colors, the textures and the perfume—breathe them in. The grass is a vivid green and the sky a beautiful blue with little white fluffy clouds. It is very peaceful in your garden; it is full of love and harmony.

> You may feel this prelude is very long but it is wise to create with care, thought and feeling the scene your child is entering. When your child is used to it, the prelude may become shorter, as it is not always necessary to describe the Star and the Angel in such full detail. Then it becomes something like the shorter version below.

I want you to see above your head a beautiful, beautiful Star. This Star is filled with lovely white light. I want you to bring the white light from that star right down through your body until you can feel it in every part of you, and your heart is filled with love for all humanity and for all creatures great and small.

Your Guardian Angel is waiting for you to

wrap a golden cloak of protection around you and take you to the Worry Tree. Put anything that worries you on the tree and then your Guardian will open the gate and take you inside your garden.

Your garden is filled with glorious flowers, the grass and the trees are an emerald green, and the sky a deep blue with white clouds.

After you have set the scene, as it were, you can do anything with the children that you think they would enjoy. Become a child again yourself—I think you will be surprised at what pleasure these flights of fantasy will give you.

The meditations in this book have been done for children of all ages. I have incorporated different themes that I feel will appeal to both the adult and the child. Indeed, some of these meditations you may care to use for yourself.

Some of the meditations I have done follow.

The Moonbeam and the Moon

YOUR GARDEN is especially beautiful as you enter. It is quiet, so quiet you could hear a mouse if it crept past you. The flowers are very proudly standing with their heads tilted back to receive the light which is bathing your garden. It is streaming down from the full moon which hangs in the sky. The branches of the trees are gently moving the moon's light through their greenery until their pearly fingers touch the ground.

Grandfather Tree is looking especially beautiful in the moonlight. The light breeze is drifting through his branches, rustling his green leaves, and the sound is like music.

As you go near the trunk of Grandfather Tree, the light from the moon becomes stronger and stronger. The moon is sending shafts of light out over the world so that everyone can see in the night, but there is a beam of light appearing at the wise old tree's feet. This light is your own special moonbeam that will take you high above the earth to the moon.

If you stand on the moonbeam, you will find it is filled with glitter, little sprinkles of which are touching all parts of your body and making it glow.

Grandfather Tree is waving goodbye as the moonbeam lifts you gently from the earth. As you rise above your garden, the flowers also wave their heads, sending their perfume high into the air.

Your moonbeam is like a finger of pure light streaming across the skies as it takes you higher and higher, lifting you further than you have been before, until you are within reach of this golden moon which has always sent its light to you from above. You can now step onto the moon, feeling its surface beneath your feet. It feels different to the earth. It feels light, and your feet skim quickly across the moon's surface. You can float and turn cartwheels as everything that lives on the moon is so light.

The Moon people are coming to greet you. They are very tall, with slender bodies, and their golden garments shine as they move. They want to take you to see the waters of the moon so that you can swim there with the beautiful moon creatures.

These Moon people want to take you to the other side of the moon, the side that they normally do not show to people. Would you like to go with them? Or perhaps you would like to see what else there is on this side first.

You can always use your special moonbeam to come here whenever you like from your garden. Just look towards the moon and ask for your own special ray of light to take you. I shall leave you now to walk on the moon...

The Snowflakes

YOU CAN feel the peace and quiet in your garden. The sky is a brilliant blue and the trees are now white with snow hanging from their branches. There are light snowflakes falling against your face. They are settling on your skin, touching it gently, and inside you feel alive and warm and wonderful.

Why don't you stand with your arms

outstretched and the snow will settle on your body. You can feel the top of your head getting taller and taller as the snow makes a huge hat. Your shoulders are growing bigger and bigger and your whole body is being covered by the gently falling flakes. Watch them coming down from the sky, forming a blanket over the trees and the houses, as well as yourself.

The snow around your body is becoming thicker and thicker. The children coming over cannot recognize you as the snow is hiding your features. They are laughing and saying they will make you into a marvellous snowman. They are patting and stroking the snow around you, rounding out some parts and flattening others. One child is placing her red and green knitted hat on your head, and another is putting a bright yellow and green knitted scarf around your neck.

Isn't it fun to be inside the snow and to be alive? The children are dancing around you and they are singing, but they do not realize that the snowman they have made can also sing and dance.

Why don't you surprise them and join them in their games? They will certainly be surprised when you move. Try moving an arm first and see if they notice anything different. Move a leg. Wink at them. And then...you could chase them.

It will be such fun to play hide-and-seek as they race through the trees. Go and play, see if you can catch them. Perhaps you could have a snowball fight...

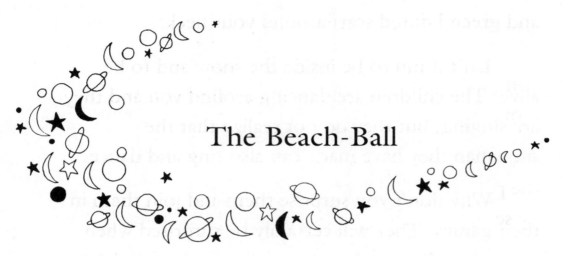

The Beach-Ball

YOU CAN feel the clean air touching your face
as you enter your garden and you can hear the
sound of waves breaking. I wonder where this
sound is coming from? If you go further down the
pathway, you will come to a beach which has lovely
clean white sand. It's not really white, mind you. It
is more of a light yellow, but because the sun is
streaming onto these tiny particles, it makes it seem

pure white. Feel the sand between your toes as you walk along carrying your shoes. It feels good to crunch through the sand and to leave your footprints behind you.

The water is a deep, deep blue highlighted by the paler blue of the sky. The sea is showing itself off by sending in large waves that thunder and curl with white foam at the top. These waves seem so high and yet, as they approach the sand, they become smaller and smaller, until they are just a trickle.

Why don't you sit on the sand and watch the waves for a while? Put some sunburn cream on your skin and rub it in gently, making sure you are fully protected from the sun's rays.

The sun is warming your body. It makes you

feel good. The sun loves to come down and spread its glow across the earth. You can hear the sound of the sea-gulls as they swoop over the water. They can be so noisy and inquisitive. If you sit quietly, you will find that some of these gulls will come close to you. You have some bread in your bag. Why don't you give them some crumbs because gulls are always hungry?

What's that I see coming in on the top of a wave? Why, it's a brightly colored beach-ball bobbing up and down. Go to the edge of the water and wait for the wave to toss it to you. The sea wants to play with you. Toss it back to the new wave coming in and it will take the ball away, but then the next wave will bring it back and throw it to you again.

When you are tired of playing, you can keep the ball. It is a present from the sea, especially for you…

The Rabbit

IN YOUR garden you can feel the warmth of the sun surrounding your body and you can smell the lovely perfume that is coming from the golden daffodils nearby. They are standing tall and straight, very proudly sending their aroma to the surrounding trees and flowers.

Standing near the daffodils is a large russet

colored rabbit. She looks a little surprised that you have entered her domain. Her ears are pricked up and her right paw is about to scratch her nose.

I wonder what her name is? I think I shall call her Mrs Rabbit. She's waving to you, asking you to close the gate behind you. As you go closer, you will see she is holding out her paw. Why don't you take it in your hand?

It does seem funny to hop along, doesn't it? It takes a little while to get into the rhythm of hopping, but once you have the hang of it, it's great fun. She's smiling because sometimes when she hops up, you go down. Keep trying to stay in time with her and, there you are, you are both hopping together.

Mrs Rabbit is taking you into her burrow where she lives with her large family. You will notice as you go down that there are passageways going every which way. She knows where she is going though. She is stopping in front of a red door with a green handle which she pushes to open. As the door opens, her many children rush to greet the two of you.

Mr Rabbit is stirring some carrot soup that he has made for their lunch. The large wooden table is set with an extra plate. He knew Mrs Rabbit would bring you with her and they are delighted that you are staying with them for a time.

The rabbit children are running around excitedly. It is the first time they have had a human visit them in their burrow.

Why don't you sit down and eat with them? After lunch, the children will teach you many games, including hopping ones, which will be fun.

Mrs Rabbit is taking you to your chair so I shall leave you with them...

The Squirrels

THERE IS an air of excitement as you enter your garden. I wonder what can be causing it? The flowers are bending their heads towards each other and the trees are waving their branches in the light breeze. You can hear a lot of chattering as you go down your pathway towards the large tree whose branches are laden with nuts.

The chattering is coming from the squirrels. They are very busy as they rush around collecting as many nuts as they can to store away. They love to hoard food in their favorite tree.

Squirrels always make sure they have enough food stored away in their larder in case they have unexpected company, like yourself.

They have long, curly tails and bright eyes and they are chattering to you in squirrel language. I am sure if you listen quietly, you will be able to understand and talk to them.

You can help pick the nuts and take them to the hole in the trunk of the tree. This is where they plan to keep their food for the next few weeks. If it is difficult for you to climb the tree, you could put on the squirrel suit they are handing you. Run your hand, or your paw, over your fur. It is thick and soft and lovely to touch.

Take some nuts in your paws and, clutching them to your furry chest, run quickly up the tree. There are squirrels everywhere you look, all busily running, all busily collecting, and placing the food into the trunk of the tree.

Mrs Squirrel is organizing the storage cupboard. As the nuts arrive, she is placing some of them into drawers, some on benches, and others into a large pot. She is making nut stew and also some nut cakes to eat later on.

Run up and down the tree trunk a few more times. If you go along the branch, you will meet a possum who is hanging upside down by his tail. That looks like a bit of fun, doesn't it? Look at the fur suit you are wearing as the squirrel and *"wish"* yourself into a suit like the possum so that you too can hang upside down. Don't things look different now that you are no longer upright?

The possum is going to eat with the squirrels when Mrs Squirrel's food is ready. You can go there as either a possum or a squirrel, or yourself, whichever you prefer. You make up your own mind...

down as they rise and fall. They are taking you far, far away, away from the shore, away from the people.

Why don't you dive under the waves and swim with the fish? Because you are so far from the shore, the fish are much larger than the ones you normally see.

There are whales and dolphins swimming lazily around you. Look at the octopus. Its arms are waving in the water. You could swim from one arm to another and count them if you want. I wonder how many arms an octopus has? He has a very large face and, do you know, I believe he is smiling at you.

Why don't you smile back? I think if you do,

Mr Octopus will take you deep into the ocean to meet his family. As he puts one of his arms around you and dives underneath the water, you will find it is easy to breathe. You don't need a mask or goggles as this water is special and you can breathe naturally.

Mrs Octopus is always busy with her five babies. She would love to have some company. The baby octopus are very small and they are waving their tiny arms at you in happiness at your arrival. They have never had a child visit them before. You can sit and eat with them at their table on the ocean floor.

There are small golden fish swimming by and the seaweed is moving gently in the water. There are little crabs crawling on the ocean floor and some of

gentle sounds as they murmur to each other.

The sea looks very inviting. Why don't you run across the sand and fall into the waves. The sun is warming your body as you swim through the clear, clean water. The waves are lifting you up and down as you go out to sea, further than you have ever been before. The sea will protect you and cushion your body with the swell of the water. Just lie there and let the water do the work until you feel you are far enough out to explore what the deeper waters hold.

Look, there are six dolphins coming towards you and they are very playful. They are darting around each other with lovely wide smiles. They are making small sounds, which is how they communicate with each other. They are around you now and their leader would like you to climb on her back. Hold on tight as they are very fast swimmers. They are taking you to the deepest part of the ocean where the whales live. The whales are much larger than the dolphins, but they too are very graceful as they swim through the waters.

Here comes a whale who is white, not grey like the others. He is swimming lazily towards you, surrounded by the grey whales. He is opening his mouth and inviting you to swim inside. Why don't you hop from the back of the dolphin into the whale's mouth?

Hasn't he got a large tongue? Why don't you walk along his tongue until you reach the bottom of

I think you will be surprised to find that there are very special people who live there. They are called Elphinites.

The Elphinites are tiny people who live inside the bottom of the mountains. They work very hard. It takes them a long, long time to collect the things they need to furnish their homes as they are small and some things are difficult to carry.

The Elphinites have pointy noses and shining inquisitive eyes. Between their large ears they wear a green beret which matches their clothing. Their waistcoats have small diamonds instead of buttons, and their pants finish just below their knees, over the tops of their red socks. Their yellow shoes curl up at the toes and they are tied with red laces.

Elphinites love to make things. Some of them are carpenters and some are painters. There are dressmakers and doll-makers, ones who like to cook, ones who like to dance. They all work together in what they do.

Their work-benches are deep in the mountain. They are lit by the light which streams down from the mountain's top. The Elphinites have built a tunnel from the bottom of the mountain to the top so they can use the sun's light to work by, and the moon's rays to sleep with.

You might like to help them. There are many things you could do. You could learn to carve wood and make toys or furniture. You could learn to cook or to sew. Or to paint. You can do whatever you

As you go down the pathway, take time to look at all the pigeons strutting around, with their chests proudly puffed out. Perhaps you could feed the bread in your bag to the pigeons. They love being fed. The butterflies' wings tickle as they land on your head and make you laugh. Some of the butterflies have huge wings for such small bodies and they are all the colors of the rainbow.

Grandfather Tree is waving to you. He has many branches and they are heavily laden with rich green leaves. I think there is someone hiding in the tree. Why don't you take a look?

Can you see who's there? Why, it's a doll, the most wonderful doll you could ever imagine. Why don't you pick it up and give it a cuddle? It must be marvellous to be a doll and to be cuddled and loved.

The doll has big bright eyes, short curly hair, and a very cheeky expression.

Grandfather Tree is waving another branch at you and this branch is full of dolls' clothing. You could select a few things so that you can dress your doll any way you would like. There are pairs of small shoes and many dresses, overalls and shirts in bright colors, wonderful scarves, sunglasses and a box filled with amazing hats.

Why don't you sit on one of Grandfather Tree's roots, which makes a lovely seat, and then you could dress your doll in the clothing you have chosen? Put the rest back on Grandfather Tree's branches for the next time you visit him.

Perhaps you could think of a name for your doll as you sit and nurse it. Would you like to call it Kris? Or Eleanor? Or Georgie? Or Robin? Or Sam? Oh dear, there are so many names to choose from that I shall just leave you to choose the one you like the most.

Grandfather Tree is hiding something at the back of his trunk. He is smiling as you walk around to see what it is. Why, it's a cradle. You could put your doll inside and push the cradle until the doll falls asleep. You could even sing a song if you like. As you watch, the doll's eyes slowly close.

I wonder if this special doll will come to life? I think that as you watch, you might find the doll is changing and becoming a little child. What do you think? Would you like it to be a little child to play with, or would you rather it stayed a doll that you could carry around? I shall leave you there to think about it...

The Circus

THERE IS a lot of excitement in your garden. Can you feel it? The trees are shaking their branches and the flowers are nodding their heads as you pass by. I wonder what is happening? You will have to go further down the path to find out. I hear laughter and I am sure that when you walk around that big tree down there, you will find out where this is coming from. I hear strange music and this music reminds me of ... *The Circus*!

How exciting to think that a circus has come to your special garden. As you go behind the tree, you will see the big top where all the special events are held. Why don't you go inside and look? They have seats going all the way around and there is a ring in the centre where the ringmaster is telling people what will happen next.

The dancing ponies are coming in first. See how their manes and tails toss as they proudly dance past to their music. The monkeys are jumping on the backs of the ponies and holding the reins, making the ponies turn in circles. The monkeys are wearing little red suits and small white hats that glitter and shine in the light as they move.

Here come the trapeze artists. They are swinging high above you, moving through the air from one side of the ring to the other. They have wonderful silver costumes on, full of beads and sequins. What a lovely feeling of freedom it must be to fly through the air and be caught by the person on the other side.

The ringmaster is now bringing out the lions. I wonder how many there are? I think there are twelve of them. Some of them have lovely manes that they toss about as they roar at the crowd. They are putting on a show for the people who are sitting on the seats, but they are not at all fierce.

I shall leave you there to enjoy the circus...

The Magician

SO MANY wonderful things happen when you are in your special garden. The air is always fresh and clean and the perfume from the flowers drifts around you. The trees bend their heads and nod to you, waving their branches excitedly as you walk along. They seem to be telling you something. If you listen carefully, you can hear what they are saying.

They are telling you that in the clearing, a little way down the path, is a magician.

Grandfather Tree is pointing the way to where the magician is. She has been waiting for you to come so that she can start her show.

She looks very grand in her sweeping black cloak with its red lining, and she wears a large black hat that she calls a top hat.

There is a table in front of her and a bird-stand nearby. She is taking her wand from the table and waving it in the air, saying the magic words "abracadabra" to make the birds appear and suddenly there are six canaries sitting on the stand and singing. I wonder how she did that? It must be the magic words and her wand.

She is going to perform another trick now. She is showing you both sides of a small colored handkerchief. She is holding it high for you to see and suddenly she starts to pull the material through her hand. It goes on and on, getting longer and longer, and each time she pulls it through, the color changes.

There is a cage behind the magician that holds a huge toy tiger with a lovely striped coat. The magician is placing a covering over the cage and she is starting to say magic words to make the tiger disappear—if you want to help her make the tiger disappear, say "abracadabra" with her and, Hey Presto!'—no tiger—and also no cage. I wonder where it has gone to?

If you stand beside her, I think she will give you her top hat and show you how to find the rabbit that lives in there. Isn't it fun to bring the white rabbit out of the hat? Be gentle though, as rabbits frighten easily.

I wonder what the magician will do next?...

The Frog

As YOU enter your garden, you hear the flowers talking to each other and the grass growing. The grass is soft underneath your feet and it springs back to life as you walk forward. The bees are going from flower to flower, and the fairies and elves dance in the clearing. As you listen, you hear a strange sound. Why don't you investigate?

Grandfather Tree is pointing in a direction you have not been before. How exciting. I wonder what is down there?

Why, it's a large pond surrounded by wildflowers of every color you could imagine. The sound you heard before is now very strong—hrumph—hrumph—hrumph. It's a frog! He is sitting on a lily pad in the pond, staring at you.

Why don't you stare back? He doesn't blink, he just sits looking at you. I would call out to him if I were you, "Frog, Frog, can I join you?"

He is smiling now and has jumped onto a larger lily pad, one that will hold the two of you. He has a small oar and is pushing it through the water to take the lily pad to where you are standing.

Hop on and sit beside the frog as he pushes off into the center of the pond. Now that you are in the center, you hear more sounds—croak, croak, croak—hrumph, hrumph, hrumph. There are a lot of frogs jumping around in the water, and some of them are choosing to bring their lily pads over so they can talk with you. "Hrumph, hrumph," they say.

Can you understand them? I think you can talk to them in their language if you like. The frog you are sitting with has a small golden crown on his head. He is called King Frog and he has a golden ball in his hand.

Why don't you become a frog for a time and then you could jump as the frogs do from lily pad to lily pad, using your strong back legs. You could join in their games. King Frog is throwing the golden ball so that you can play with it and the other frogs. It's fun, isn't it, being a frog for a change.

King Frog has a castle at the other end of the pond and it is called "Frog Mansion". He would like to take you home to meet Queen Frog and the Frog Princesses and Princes.

Take his hand, and the two of you can jump from leaf to leaf, until you reach Frog Mansion. They are going to have a sing-a-long and they have invited other frogs to come and meet you. Perhaps you can join in their singing and dancing...

The Bottle

AS YOU enter your garden, you want to dance and whirl, do cartwheels, jump for joy. The flowers are sending out a wonderful aroma that drifts around you and the grass is like a soft carpet beneath your feet. There are many small white clouds drifting across the beautiful blue sky. You could sit and watch these clouds and see what patterns they form.

The butterflies are coming forward to greet you and are flying round your head and body. Some are settling gently on your shoulders and hair.

They are whispering to you that there is someone special further down the path. If you follow them, they will take you to the right place.

The butterflies are flying together, except for the ones that have decided to stay on your head. Their colors merge with each other to create a moving rainbow as they go up and down and across each other's path.

They are taking you to a clearing surrounded by trees and bushes and white flowers that look like stars. In the center of the clearing is a plain glass bottle. Why don't you pick it up and see what is inside? I wonder why it is sitting on its own in this clearing? It must be something special just for you.

Look at it again carefully, and this time you will see a small person sitting on the bottom. I wonder how you will get him out? Close your eyes and *wish* very hard for him to appear before you.

When you open your eyes, you will see the bottle growing taller and taller, until it is the same height as yourself. The person inside has also grown and is now opening the doorway of the bottle and stepping outside onto the grass to be with you.

He is dressed in green with green pointy shoes that have yellow pom poms on them. He is wearing a large pair of red glasses and his green hat, also with a yellow pom pom to match his shoes, sits at a jaunty angle on his head, dangling over one eye. His name is Merriwether.

He is so pleased you have come to see him. He loves having children come and *wish* him out of his bottle. He has a flute to play for you. Would you like to play too? Merriwether is giving you a flute so that you can play a tune together.

The music coming from your flutes attracts many animals to the clearing. The white star flowers are sitting up proud and straight and the trees are gently talking to each other, not wanting to interrupt the music.

There are all sorts of animals coming close to you. Some of them are sitting down listening, and others have decided to dance. There is an elephant dancing on her hind legs waving her trunk around as though she is conducting the music. That monkey is being a bit cheeky though—he is swinging on the elephant's tail!

The lions have brought their babies with them and the cubs are having a lovely time dancing with each other. The donkeys are kicking their heels up in the air and clicking them and some of them are dancing with the zebras.

Merriwether would like you to stay with him for a while. If you are tired of playing the flute, perhaps you might want to dance with the animals. It is up to you...

The Star Fairy

YOU CAN feel the peace and harmony in your garden. The sky is an indigo blue and the clouds are small and scattered. The sun is a rich golden yellow and spreads light dappling through the trees.

The birds are twittering, the rabbits hopping, the lions roaring, and the monkeys swing through the branches as you enter your garden. There are dogs and cats and elephants, camels and boldly colored parrots, all waiting to greet you.

They know something that you don't. The elephant is swinging you onto her back with her trunk as she ambles down the pathway that will take you to the Grandfather Tree. All the animals are following the elephant, whose short tail is swishing from side to side as she lumbers forward.

Grandfather Tree is waving his branches to you in welcome. He is very excited as there is someone special hiding in his branches. Can you see who it is? Look very carefully between the leaves and you will see the Star Fairy.

Isn't she beautiful? Her dress is silver and is made of fine material that shimmers in the sunlight.

Her wings look as though cobwebs of silver have been woven through them, and on her head she wears a silver star that shines brilliantly.

She is smiling in welcome as she has waited a long time to meet you. She sees you bring the light from the star through your body before you enter your garden and she is always delighted to watch what you do when you are there.

She is taking you by the hand and lifting you from the earth. Wave goodbye to Grandfather Tree and the animals as the Star Fairy is taking you to her home in Starland. You will see your garden becoming smaller and smaller as you rise above the earth and it becomes but a dot as you move farther and farther away.

You feel safe and secure with the Star Fairy as you fly towards Starland. You are both hovering above the stars until the Star Fairy glides down towards the one that belongs to her.

Everything glistens and gleams on her star. And, look, other Star Fairies are coming to meet you. Each Star Fairy looks after a particular child but they always like to meet the others who belong to their friends.

They are taking you to the lighthouse that beams the light of the stars towards earth. There are many beams lighting up the sky and the light is brilliant where you are, but it becomes less bright when it reaches the earth.

You can enter the lighthouse if you like and

discover how the light is made. I am sure the Star Fairy will allow you to direct the light of your special star towards your house so that your family feel this light. Why don't you mix lots of star-dust with it? It would form a blanket over your home that would twinkle in the night for all to see.

Your Star Fairy will take you to other stars so that you can meet the fairies that live there. If you ask, perhaps they will show you the children they look after. I shall leave you there in Starland...

The Brown Bears

THE SUN is warming your body as you wander through your garden, feeling the warmth and peace there. Feel the freshness of the air against your skin and breathe it in, feel it cleaning your lungs. You can now smell something quite different. I wonder what it can be? Why, I think it is honey.

There are many bees around and they are

flying in a straight line towards a large green tree in the distance. Why don't you follow these bees and find out what they are doing? If you listen carefully, you can hear them calling to each other that they must hurry back to their hive.

One of the larger bees is landing in front of you and asking you to climb on his back. If you settle down between his wings, he will give you a ride there.

Doesn't this bee go fast? The green of the trees and the colors of the flowers become a blur as he speeds towards the hive. He is slowing down now that he is within landing distance and he is calling out to someone who is standing by the big tree.

Why, I do declare, it is a v-e-r-y large brown

grizzly bear. In fact, when I look there are two of them.

The bees are settling down around their hive where their Queen lives. They are asking the bears to hand them the honey-pot if they want some honey, and they will fill it up.

The bees cannot stay long as they have to get back to work. The flowers have prepared the pollen to give to the bees. It gets very heavy if they have to hold it too long. The bees need to bring the pollen back to the hive for their Queen so that more honey can be made.

The grizzly bear is picking you up in its large paws. It is being careful to hold you away from the honey as it goes around the tree to take its mate home. They would like to take you to their cave as their children have never seen someone like you before.

Would you like to go? It feels nice having the soft brown fur against your face, and the huge arms around you. The bears' cave is not far from the tree where the hive is. As you approach it, there are three little balls of brown fur tumbling over each other, each wanting to be the very first to reach you. And they are longing to play with you.

But first, why don't you have lunch with this bear family? There is honey bread and honeycomb to eat and a drink which is honey nectar...

The Polar Bears

YOUR GARDEN is full of excitement, even the trees seem to be moving more than usual. There are many birds in the sky and some of them come to land on the Grandfather Tree. He is beckoning to you to come near his large trunk so that he can bend to whisper in your ear.

"You have been to so many other places that

have been exciting but have you ever thought about going to the Arctic? The Arctic is v-e-r-y, v-e-r-y different and I think now is the time to go. Walk towards the pier and you will find a large black and white ship in front of you. It is preparing to go there. Why don't you climb the gangway as they are expecting you to join them?"

The boat is surging forward, pushing the sea onto either side of it. It is going up and down, up and down. Isn't it great? It is a bit difficult to walk at first with the motion of the boat, but it does not take long before you have the hang of it.

The ice is building up in the water as the ship goes further toward the Arctic. There are h-u-g-e blocks of ice floating past. If you put your hand out, carefully of course, you could touch one of them. It is cold to the touch, isn't it?

The boat's captain has asked if you would like to take the wheel and steer the boat through the water. Would you like to do that? Be careful of the floating ice and take the boat around it so that you don't scrape the boat's sides.

The captain is telling you to land the boat. You are far enough into the Arctic Circle that the ice is firm to walk on. Guide the boat to the iced jetty where it can be moored while you get off and stretch your legs.

Why don't you join the captain and the crew and walk across the ice?

Can you see that marvellous creature? It is big and white and beautiful. Do you know, I think it is a polar bear. It is standing on its hind legs and waving its front paws for you to come closer. As you go over, you will feel you are skating on the ice. You could even do a pirouette if you like.

The polar bear is taking you by the hand as you skate, pointing out where the seals live. Oh, do look at them. Aren't they beautiful in their sleek suits? There are so many of them. Some of them are lying together, while others are gliding in and out of the water for a swim.

They are swimming with lots of other animals. Why, they are walruses! Aren't the walruses noisy when they talk to each other?

The polar bear will introduce you to the seals and walruses. When you are finished talking with them, the bear will take you home to meet its family and to eat something. Would you like that?

The captain and crew will wait to bring you back. Take your time with the polar bear. There is no hurry...

England

THE SUN is a huge golden ball in the sky as you enter your garden. The sky is a crystalline blue with a tinge of purple, and there are small white clouds scudding by.

As you look at these clouds, it makes you want to join them. Why don't you? You don't need a plane nor a rocket on your back. Look down at your feet and you will see them rising above the grass, taking you higher and higher, until you are floating above the earth. If you like, you could catch a cloud that would take you to England, or you could fly there yourself.

When you reach England you could look for a suitable landing spot near Buckingham Palace where the Queen lives. Why don't you land there? I wonder if the Queen is inside at the moment? Perhaps she is at Parliament House or at her favorite home, Sandringham.

Knock on the door and when the butler opens it, ask politely if it is possible to see the Queen. He smiles and nods his head before taking you through some stately rooms, beautifully furnished with large pieces of furniture. There are many paintings on the walls, enough to fill an art gallery.

The butler is taking you into the Queen's reception area where she is waiting to greet you. She has a lovely open smile, full of warmth, and she is extending her hand to you. She will take you on a tour of the palace, showing you where they sleep, where they study and work, and she will even take you down to the kitchens, which have many pots and pans and utensils.

The Queen must hurry now as she is due at Parliament House to meet her Ministers. You can go with her if you wish. Her horse-drawn carriage is pulling up at the door and the footman is helping both the Queen and yourself into the carriage.

There are many people outside the gates of Buckingham Palace who are cheering the Queen. You too can wave as the carriage draws away.

Why don't you wave and smile to the people who are waiting outside Parliament House? The Queen is getting out of the carriage and is holding her hand out to you. She is smiling at the look on your face as you see this old historic building. You could go inside and listen to Parliament debating the issues of government, while the Queen makes decisions with her Ministers.

When it is over, you can have afternoon tea with the Queen and her corgis before it is time for her to depart for an important social occasion. Give her a kiss on the cheek as she leaves and wave the carriage goodbye.

You could go for a walk as there are many things to see in London, such as Big Ben, the Charles Dickens shop, Westminster Cathedral, or the Tower of London with the guards who wear such strange hats and are called Beefeaters.

London Bridge is nearby. Why not go there and watch the boats on the Thames River? You may even decide to ride in a boat and relax as it takes you around London's waterway...

The White House

I FEEL AS though you want to travel, to take off into the wide blue sky that stretches over your garden. Feel yourself leaving the ground and flying through the air. You could use wings or fly through space using your mind to take you there. Because you often fly your own way, why don't you ride on a large aeroplane this time.

Ask one of the cabin staff if you can go forward to where the captain sits. He may allow you to sit in the cabin and watch as the plane flies over the countryside. He will point out different things on the control panel and will help you to understand the computerised operation of the plane. The captain has said you could fly the plane if you like.

You can choose where you would like to go. You could fly over the Statue of Liberty which is outside New York. Isn't she huge? You can make the plane dip just over her head and then pull back up towards the sky. You could stop and visit if you want.

When you decide to move on, settle down at

the plane's controls, looking at the maps, and select a city you would really like to visit. I feel there is someone waiting for you.

Look below at that large white building and, yes, I do believe that it is the White House in Washington. This is where the President lives.

There are people standing on the lawn and they are waving to you with hankies and scarves. Why don't you bring the plane down at the airfield nearby? The President has sent a car to pick you up and bring you to the White House.

The big car has all sorts of things inside. There is a color television, stereo music, and if you feel hungry, look in the small fridge. You are so excited that all you want to do is reach that white building and meet the people who live there.

The car is taking you through the gate and is going up the driveway where the President and his wife are waiting to greet you. The building has been freshly painted and gleams in the sunlight.

Mr and Mrs President are taking you inside the White House. It has high ceilings and the rooms are large enough for a party with hundreds of people.

Why don't you run ahead and play hide-and-seek with Mr and Mrs President? They love children and would like to play with you.

This building holds many secret places to hide and play in. They will show you some of the places you can go but you must find the rest. There is a room just for children, which is special for each child who visits. It has all the things they have ever wished for, and some they haven't even thought of.

Would you like to take Mr and Mrs President by the hand and go with them to your special room? I think they would enjoy going with you as they are really children themselves inside—they just seem to be grown-up.

And when it is time for afternoon tea, why don't you slide down the banisters all the way to the dining room? That is always fun. In fact, I think Mr and Mrs President's grandchildren like to do that too.

Afternoon tea is full of surprises. Small cakes with pink icing, sausage rolls, and chocolates that

will delight you. After you have eaten, you may
want to play again. Or go sliding on the banisters
once more. I will leave it up to you...

Disneyland

THE ROSES are blooming in your garden and their fragrant perfume is wafting through the air. There is a gentle breeze blowing and your own special white cloud is drifting down to earth. You have used this cloud before as it often comes to your garden. It has a set of gossamer reins and a small seat to hold you comfortably as you take off into the air.

Sometimes you visit the Cloud People on Mother Cloud, but this time your cloud is taking you somewhere else. I wonder where it is?

The cloud is flying very fast. In the distance you can see many buildings of strange shapes and sizes. But look, there is one that looks like a castle. I am sure you have seen this castle before in books, in films, or on TV. It looks like a magic castle to me and I feel this magic castle belongs to... D-I-S-N-E-Y-L-A-N-D!!!

Oh, isn't it exciting. Your small white cloud is bringing you into the grounds of Disneyland now. Very gently you land inside the front gates.

Can you see who is waiting for you? Why, it is Minnie Mouse and Mickey Mouse. They are much larger than you imagined, aren't they? And they do have very large ears! They are taking you by the hand, one on either side, as they want you to meet some of their other friends.

Here comes Goofy. He's saying, "Gawrsh, I'm glad to meetcha" as he shakes your hand. He is surprised to see your cloud hovering nearby. He has never seen a cloud bring a child to Disneyland before.

Oh my, can you hear that—Quack—Quack—Quack. It's Donald—Donald Duck that is. And he has his three nephews with him, Huey, Dewey and Louie. And his girlfriend, Daisy, is coming over to welcome you, too.

Daisy is taking you to a bed where a beautiful

girl lies. Bending over her is Prince Charming and, as he kisses her, Sleeping Beauty comes to life. She stretches her arms wide as though she has been asleep for such a long time, and smiles at you in welcome.

I hear a broom going—whisk—whisk—whisk. Can you hear it? It's Cinderella. She is still sweeping while her two large step-sisters get ready for the ball. Aren't they in for a surprise when she turns up looking beautiful with her small feet in glass slippers and wins the Prince's heart?

Her Fairy Godmother is standing alongside with her magic wand. Why don't you ask her to wave her wand for you? I wonder what will happen? Will you choose somewhere else to go within

Disneyland? Or will you choose to bring something back with you? Perhaps you will ask for both...

The Easter Eggs

YOU FEEL full of joy and happiness as you wander through your special garden. The air is fresh and the trees are whispering to each other as you pass close by. Can you hear what they are saying? Listen carefully...why, the trees are telling you that it is time to make the eggs. I hear you saying, "Eggs, what eggs?" "Why, the Easter Eggs" the trees reply.

I wonder where you go to watch these eggs being made. The big tree near you is bending over and pointing down the pathway. With a large branch, he gives you a gentle push on the small of your back to start you on your way.

The bushes are swaying in the light breeze and the flowers nod their heads to you as you pass by. Why don't you stop and smell the scent of these beautiful flowers before you go any further. They love children stopping to touch them gently.

Did you see that big rabbit go bounding by? You had better call out to him. I wonder what his name is? Why, of course, it's the *Easter Bunny*. He loves wearing the suit that looks like a draughts-board, with big squares all over it. Between his ears is a big floppy red hat that comes slightly over his left eye.

Why don't you call out to him? I think he has heard you. Why, yes, he's turning around to see where your voice is coming from. He's telling you that you are late. He has been waiting for you for such a long time.

He is taking you to a clearing where there are a lot of rabbits working over several large pots which are heated by big fires. Why don't you look inside one of these pots? Why, it is full of chocolate.

The Easter Bunny is going to show you how they prepare the eggs for Easter-time. He is going to let you make some of them too. Because the chocolate is hot, put the large spoon very carefully into the chocolate. When it is full, pour it into the egg mold until it cools. There are a lot of molds and shapes to use. You can make a lot of eggs, which will be great fun.

When the eggs have cooled and set, you can help to take them out of their shapes and wrap them in shiny paper. There is paper in all colors—red, orange, a very bright yellow, purple, green and blue.

You can place the eggs in their many baskets. The rabbits have to work hard to make sure they have enough eggs for all the children at Easter-time. I am sure they wouldn't mind if you tasted one.

And when it is time to hand the eggs out, perhaps you will return and give the Easter Bunny a hand...

The Reindeer

YOUR GARDEN is v-e-r-y quiet, even the trees seem to be standing quietly, not moving a branch. The animals are hushed, with their ears pricked up and the flowers are bending their heads as though they are hearing something you cannot. I wonder what it can be?

Listen carefully, what can you hear? I can hear

the sound of sleigh bells. They are getting louder and louder, making such a noise. R-i-n-g, r-i-n-g, r-i-n-g. I wonder where they are coming from. I cannot see anything and I am looking very carefully around me. The breeze is moving the bushes but there is no sleigh.

I wonder...Where could it be coming from? Oh yes, I see it now. It's flying through the sky and about to land on the ground in front of you. It's a beautiful sleigh pulled by eight reindeer, but there is no driver.

The reindeer are prancing around as they wait for you to get into the driver's seat and to take the leather reins in your hands. They are going to take you away from the earth and into the heavens, flying higher and higher until they go past the moon and the sun and the other planets.

I think they are preparing to land now. Yes, they are slowing down and drifting towards a small cottage with farm buildings close by. There are two people waiting for the sleigh to settle firmly on the ground. They are both jolly people, rather large around their middles. Their names are Mr and Mrs Santa Claus.

Although it's not Christmas yet, they sent their reindeer to find you. They thought you might like to spend some time with them. They would like to show you the factory where the toys are made.

Santa has you by one hand and Mrs Claus by the other as they take you into the building where the toys are. This building is divided into sections. One is where the toys are made, another where they are painted, another where the broken ones are mended. You can see some people writing books and then printing them. Some are weaving hair for the many dolls which are all around.

Perhaps you would like to help with the Christmas preparations...and maybe when it is the right time, you may return and help Santa distribute the presents...

The Yellow School-House

THE FLOWERS are dressed in their prettiest colors as you enter your garden. They are sitting tall and proud, sending their perfume wafting through the leaves on the bushes and into the branches of the trees. As you go down your garden path, feeling the warmth of the earth beneath your feet, you will come to the Grandfather Tree. The Grandfather Tree is the oldest tree in your garden and he has a lot of knowledge and wisdom.

The Grandfather Tree is pointing to a small building across the clearing. He is saying that this is where you get your own knowledge and wisdom. It is a school house which has been painted a golden yellow with a bright red door.

Why don't you turn the handle on the red door and go inside? There are a lot of small desks with chairs that just fit underneath and there is a blackboard in front of them with chalk on the ledge below. Why don't you pick up the chalk and draw someone you would like as a teacher?

Teachers like to show you how to do things. They love it when you show them how much you want to learn. Some teachers like to teach mathematics by making it a game. Then it becomes much easier to learn how to put the numbers together.

Other teachers love to speak about writing stories, where to put the right words and how to spell them, but especially, how to use your imagination. Why don't you think of stories you would really like to put on paper? You could write about anything you like.

You could do a lot of things in this school room. I shall leave you there to do what you want...

School and the Grandfather Tree

THE AIR is fresh and cool and the slight wind ruffles your hair as you enter your garden. The sun is high in the sky and the white clouds float gently overhead. Some of the leaves from the trees have fallen to the earth creating a carpet for you to walk on.

Grandfather Tree has been waiting to talk to

you. He loves having children visit him and sit at his feet. He would like to talk to you about what you can learn in school and how exciting it can be to learn about history and geography.

He says that history tells us about people's lives: how they lived; where they lived; their families. History speaks to us of kings and queens, people who fought for what they believed in, of doctors who discovered medicines and cures for illness that no one else had found. History tells us many, many things. Of pharaohs who lived in Egypt near the Nile, of popes who lived in the Vatican City in Rome, Italy, of people who left their homes and sailed around the world and found new countries.

Geography makes us want to travel. Have you

thought of the many places you can go in this world? Why, there is Egypt with its pyramids and camels, Africa with its exotic animals, Australia with its koalas and kangaroos, America with the Statue of Liberty and the buffalo, Japan with its temples and cherry blossom and China with its Great Wall. These countries are known for many other things, which makes you want to visit them.

If you put history and geography together, you could write a marvellous story.

I wonder what you will choose to do?...

Also by Maureen Garth — Starbright

Driven by the desire to help her three-year-old daughter settle down into a peaceful night's sleep, Maureen Garth devised meditations that would help her daughter feel secure and cared for. *Starbright* is a collection of the stories Garth created as her child grew older. These innovative meditations are simple visualisations parents and teachers can read to their children to help them sleep, develop concentration, awaken creativity, and learn to quiet themselves.

In her engaging, warm, and personal style, Garth teaches parents how to help their children relax, concentrate, and develop artistic and mental abilities, as well as enjoy a good night's sleep.

MAUREEN GARTH was an innovative teacher and writer who lived in Sydney, Australia. Maureen has written three further books of meditations for children, *Moonbeam, Sunshine* and *Earthlight*. She has also written books for older readers, including *The Power of the Inner Self*: a book of visualisations created to fire the imagination, bring peace and healing to the body, and comfort the soul, and *Innerspace*: a collection of creative visualisations to help teenagers meet the challenges of adolescence.

ISBN 1 86371 206 2